Introduction

New Poets Ten continues the tradition of Friendly Street introducing new and emerging poets into the stratosphere of the Australian poetry community. On the Friendly Street launch pad three poets, Libby Angel, Rob Bloomfield and Rob Walker, prepare for lift off. Bleak intimacies share cabin space with formalism, surrealism, Augustan satire, sprawling parody and sharp observations of the natural world.

But this is also a passenger flight, so buy your tickets and climb aboard. The view will astound you as the words of these three poets fall to earth like fresh rain.

Gaetano Aiello
Convenor
Friendly Street 2005

friendly street
NEW POETS TEN

stealing libby angel

deaf elegies robert j bloomfield

sparrow in an airport rob walker

Friendly Street Poets

Wakefield Press

Friendly Street Poets Incorporated
in association with
Wakefield Press
1 The Parade West
Kent Town
South Australia 5067

www.friendlystreetpoets.org.au
www.wakefieldpress.com.au

First published 2005

Cover design and photography by Ben Walker
Typeset by Clinton Ellicott, Wakefield Press
Printed and bound by Hyde Park Press, Adelaide

ISBN 1 86254 670 3

  Friendly Street is supported by the
South Australian Government
Government
of South Australia   A R T S A   through Arts South Australia.

 Wakefield Press thanks Fox Creek Wines
Fox Creek   and Arts South Australia for their support.
Wines

Contents

Stealing

by *Libby Angel*

Born in the dawn of the seventies,
Libby Angel lived in Melbourne, London and
Cuba, making a scant living as an aerialist
before re-emerging in Adelaide to complete
an Honours degree in Creative Writing at
Flinders University. She recently performed
as part of the Weimar Room Adelaide
Cabaret Fringe 2004.

Acknowledgements

'The white dress' and a version of 'Distress Shop' were published in *Hecate*, 29.2.2003. 'Dragged' was accepted for publication in the February 2005 issue of *Overland* and 'Ineligible' was accepted for the 2004 issue of the *Friendly Street Reader*.

Contents

I snatched a man

out of the winter air. He drove me in the blue car, wobbling and
rattling through the dark backstreets of the town, past decaying
cottages with tatty curtains, tumbledown chimneys, picket fences
crooked as teeth. Skinny cats skit across alleyways. We rolled into
the driveway of an old house and stammered through the fly-
screen door. A wind-chime shattered the breeze. A clipped static
voice shot out of a radio in the corner. It was 4 am. The chairs
crumbled beneath our bones, the dry hum of a heater blew at our
feet. We drank black tea with lemons from a spiky tree. Stories
wound out of the man's mouth through the tall, dark, empty
rooms, into the cracks in the walls. A gangster in a suit sat down,
fanned a winning hand of cards. A woman in lace spilled across
the floor, a square bottle of scotch in her skinny grip, a dark smile
smeared across her pale living face. The house creaked like a ship. I
floated on the man's voice across the seven seas and flew with
laughter through the infinite galaxies. He talked so fast his mouth
began to smoke like a gun. I wanted to kiss that mouth with the
stories in it and never return to these shores.

For Mick

Imbolc (1)

Olive branches scratch the fog.
Birds stand mute, feather-wet in silver caves
dreaming eggs, drafting soft thatch.
The lemon tree whinges on the tin.
Urgent with dawn, possums lump and roll
their tackle of thorny fruit.
The pink sun stills them
then the quiet carousel fades out of town.
Priests peal awake, all creatures surface from sleep.
Clouds glower in the Sunday grass &
through a scribble of black sticks,
morning dribbles in.

Imbolc (2)

I have seen the resurrection
of trees, rot washed clean and
other miracles. I have stirred the living mud
& spied its craft. Amidst the violent architecture
of roots, worms make alchemy of death,
mouthing damp rumours concerning the sun.
The days, more graceful now, bow their smiles
against night. New leaves grow
unabashed. Every bush offers its sticky brides
to the light & now the bees must soldier them.
Happiness is our people's duty.

Imbolc (3)

The sun is unwelcome here.
Even the shadows burn.
The hills are bald, trees
peel & crackle, fruit shrivels
in its skin. Ants march
to their loot, nothing else moves.
Sun crashes through lidless sky,
the ground swells with our feet.
Afternoons are as lonely as the moon.

The periodontist

straddles me in the surgery chair, slaps on his spanky latex gloves,
wiggles my jagged teeth in my silly head. Do you know how to
clean your teeth, he says, and stretches my lips like labour, knuckly
gold rings frottaging my cheeks. *Vogue* slips from my lap like silk,
splats on the sterile floor. He skewers his booster needle deep into
my pink bones. The pleasantries swell in my mouth. I gag on his
cologne. A designer nurse with a bleachy smile blots my tears with
a tissue as they roll like clouds of thunder down my plain face.
Then the periodontist begins. He lances my gums, drills, sucks,
blows, scrapes, wrenches, picks, his dandy crocodile loafers tapping
to the music. I spit green antiseptic on demand, watch it froth and
swirl into the steel clinical sink. He wedges pastel bandages into
my fat mouth, sews me up like a gummy old doll. Ejected from
my seat, I stagger numbly to reception and pay, pay, pay, so my
teeth may lie pearly in my grave and my periodontist may live
a bit.

Fantasy in Dirt

I heaved a watermelon
to their party, a juicy
and fecund invocation:
IVF au naturel.

I sat, an untenable fantasy in dirt.
He moved to better view
my legs, long as famous summer.

I watched his hands
plough the cake hot silt.
The tomatoes flamed
on their stalks.

We stood on the track.
Streamer leaves shook off
light, the brown dam shivered.
Summer keeled in the wind.

Ghosts rattled me in the guest bed,
sucking his wife through cold
rooms. Owls spoke intrigue
through the curtains.

In unwelcome morning,
magpies stole my song.
She grew smug fruit
I, redundant.

Veronica Visits Coolart

Everything was old. The stables and the carts, the rusted chains
and the black trees. The music was old. Sepia men with beards and
sticks and hats hung on the walls. They called them the settlers.
They were so old they were dead. The walls were old, the polished
furniture and the china, the glazed jugs in their basins. The
kitchen was dark and stale. There were free cups of tea from an
urn; chamomile. The quilting society had a noticeboard; hessian.
I wrote in the visitors' book but I could not concentrate. I wrote
outside the lines. There were many rooms, many rooms were
locked. We wanted to see those old, locked rooms. The doors were
newly glossed. We ran down the stairs. The stairs were old, of
course, and spongy. We ran outside, we danced like puppets
through fields of corn. The music drugged us, our feet were
young, the brass band made us jump and run. The people were
old. They played old violins in white marquees and brushed their
shiny drums. They were swing time people. They sat, folded up in
deck chairs by the roses, sipping wine or dancing politely in pairs.
The roses, too, were old. We ate lemon slice with icing. We did
not drink. Even we were older than before. We laughed for a
thousand years.

For V

Ineligible

Once again the vernal bachelors have passed.
I am not so denim as the chosen ones who dip
their lovely fingers in, nor do I know
how to command a man and his socks. Furthermore,
my father has left me a dowry of unpleasant things.
Once, I tried to walk where twelve roses would snare my hem.
I met some odd shapes in the dark and other sunken folk.
A blank man stole my cherries. Then, one spring day
I met myself and disappeared in dust from my shelf.

Clean

If I was a proper lady, I would have a sucky vacuum cleaner and I
would suck up dust. The drains wouldn't stink of rotting meat,
the lino would not be sticky, nor adrift from the boards. The mice
in the floor would not be giggling, would not be screaming in
shredded nests of crumbs and fluff and paper and dust, would not
be shitting in the saucepans. The gutters would flow freely and it
would not rain inside. The weeds would not strangle the flowers.
The shower would not be slippery, the tiles not slick nor sullied
with slime. The bath would be pleasant blue, the fridge and oven
white. They would reflect a perfect smile. The windows would not
be smeared in grease, nor fat spat over the walls. No bugs would
besmirch the carpet nor burrow into the couch. No ink stains, no
chocolate stains, no tea stains, no dog stains, no blood would stain
my sheets, my carpet, my couch. My sheets would be new, folded
flat as paper, not second-hand second-feet where other people
cried and slept and died and wept and left their memory stains.
If I was a proper lady, I would not lie where others' heads have
thought their dirty thoughts and I would not be intimate with
strangers' imprints and their pre-loved dreams. My pillows would
be antibacterial. I would have a washing machine that whirls and
gushes and foams and washes the dirt away, spinning it out of
existence. I would have a witchy scratchy broom, a bristly
scrubbing brush, a pair of thick pink rubber gripping gloves, a
squidgy squeezy mop and a plastic bucket that is red. I would have
some neck-snapping mouse-traps that hide in the dark, a party
pack of rat sack, a bottle of killer bleach and a blue frothy toilet so
clean it would burn the sinuses out of your head. The germs and
the stains and the vermin and the stink and the sticky hairs would
be gone. I am grown-up now, and I should be a proper lady.
I should be clean.

Stealing

It began a clear unnoticed weeping –
I gathered beauty through the door.

Men were pleased, satin satisfies.
The absconder wears no face.

But
I never possessed
that yellow dress.

Catalogue Life

I want a Kmart catalogue life in assorted colours and styles.
(Styles, colours and sizes will vary from store to store.)
I want a Big Fat / Stable Table / Step Stool / Twin touch lamps.
I'm talking Home Concepts. I'm talking Essential Pillows.
Warm in winter, cool in summer / Ideal for home or office /
Effective against rats, mice, spiders and cockroaches /
Ideal protection for walls and wall paper / Odourless /
Treated for allergy protection / Sanitized with a Z.
I want that which Provides extra comfort in bed /
Folds for easy storage / with Bonus collapsible dog bowl.
I want a Hot Price / Special Buy / Renewable bundle pack /
Twenty-percent extra / For less than the price of one.
I want torsos in Joanne firm support soft cup bras
and men who barbecue. 3 for $25 (pictured bras only).
I want Xtend Gel pens / Jumbo refillers / Valvoline Syn Power
injector twin-packs / Arlec Enforcer hedge trimmers.
I want Free enlargements / No negative required.
I'm talking Simple Solutions / Men's Solutions /
a 2 year old bagged bush / available in
5m domestic, side entry or piggyback lead.
Includes: game and hand-controller /

Double-sided / Single Use / Free Wet Shine.
(Restricted for sale or play to persons 15 years or over,
unless accompanied by a parent or guardian.
Props and accessories pictured are not included.)
We're always cutting you a good deal / We're cutting the cost
of living. I want to cut the cost of living a good deal.
We're passing our savings on to you.
I want to be saved. I want to GET ONE FREE.
I want a Kmart catalogue life
With safe lock mechanism.
(No rainchecks / While stocks last.)

Distress Shop

You lay your mind by in the mall, change before the
    seasons, change
from the outside in. You fit in like I never could, walk the high
    street peacock
walk. You grab the man while he is on sale, express yourself with
    your credit card.
You are the queen of billboard love, of Witchery, of the
    white Birkenstocks
in the window display, of the hyperventilating air-conditioned
    castles of
consumerism. Oh great conqueror of the cultural signifier you are
    a shopping
bag. How the piteous sweatshop poor must envy your denim
    reflection & long to scale
those escalator heights! How well you conform to the
    modern feminine
rules & how you must pity my ugliness, my holes, my
    distasteful green
op-shop sloppiness. Well I tried to be a lady but being desirable
is so costly these days & I've always had the urge to wear
    my underpants
on my sleeve. I could never zip up my damned quirks. When
    I looked
in the mirror to see if I was thin enough, I couldn't get Sudan
out of my head. It was all an anxiety attack on a hanging rack
    to me.

Dragged

I might have dragged
my pants on like you and walked
in sensible shoes through the world alone
but never conscious of it, without
referring to my own reflection
not even to straighten my tie.
I might have been dependant but
never known it. I might have found
a dumb wife to settle on my breast
pocket like a mote and she might have
kept my nose clean and consoled me
for a time. I might never have been
told that in spite of love,
dogs, children, cars, & all fortitudinous
attempts to furnish solitude, that
all meetings must end in parting.

My Mother's Wings

The wheel of fortune turns. In mourning for the sun, leaf veins
    tatter, lose grip,
drift. A spell of cool shadows lurks beyond sight. Like spiders,
death waits on the other side of corners.

My mother died in autumn. It was May. The first breath of chill
was creeping under the doors. She died with a hole in her chest.
The blood gurgled through bandages from its underworld, a
    rancid well.

They cut it out. They burnt it. They poisoned it like a rat.

Her chest concave and wounded, her heart began to decompose
in the certainty of death. She sat hunched, scared, retreating
    into feathers,
could not lie down in hurt, she said. It's hard to tell you
    how much.

The tumour clawed her throat like a succubus, stealing her
    last words.
She shrank, frowning into her ill-fit skin.

The doctor smothered her in comfort, hit her up with surrender.
Her eyes searched upward to flickering lids, her nostrils thinly
    sucked bergamot,
roses sweating and her own rotting flesh.

The candle smoked to the cornices. The space between her rattled
    breath increased.
From her empty chest of shallow bones her breath walked out into
    the world.
In our palms, she was still.

We whispered in the garden, stealing flowers. We sprinkled petals
    where she lay.
We preserved the flame. We sat holding, until it was safe to depart.

Linear time does not distance me.
The absence of flesh and blood is science.

My mother is always too close to observe with any wit.

the white dress

in the white dress I am dancing circles of flight bulbous round
happy with life at the baptism at the birthday party at the
communion I am a blushed russian temple doll with wisps of pink
and sugar hearts wishing wand shiny happy tinfoil sun at my
wedding my prince will come finally but not finally I am laid out
porcelain dead in frou frou feet hanging bare perfect glossy red
nailed cheeks rouge in the white tiered satin rose cake dress at the
ultimate floating ecclesiastical in the sky perfect for every once in a
life death eternal occasion a clear space in the clouds souls rising
up sinless red apples sparkling in celestial light winging it to the
golden gates where love waits and smiles

Seventh Day Invention

Sometimes I lie through these dreary Sundays, straight as ticking
in my cot, beneath the weight of damp feathers, the sad applause
of rain and the tinny drip of drainpipes choked with leaves and
sticks. Without ladder or man or roast lamb, I cut my own hands
and bleed in my own gutters. I am not a good woman and God
does not visit here on Sundays. Only the shrinking woman from
her watchtower comes to save my sinking soul. She mutters from
the hairy corners of her dry, devout mouth, and crams piles of
bleary printed piousness between the door and the doorstep where
the draft pushes in. The screen door crashes off its spring, the
doorbell too, is broken. Hoary knuckles rap the frosted window,
blue bone against glass. As the clatter of her hobble heels mark the
stones with her retreat, I hide in my steeple of sleep, out of
sanctity's reach.

Zoloft Dreams

My libido was a nuisance anyway.

Vaguely thrilled I lie
in my own disabled arms

while the subsidized cortex rabbit
jumps my twisting hole;

down the throat,
100mg of bitterness.

Dry-mouthed ghosts walk and
I shunt engines with my sighs,

globe-trot nightly
in setraline shoes.

The car swerves and I might die
three times a night, but I never feel a thing.

Somebody could love me
and it would not rock me

because before it ever dawns,
the reuptake inhibitor crows.

Who isn't, who am I not
to be, wired to the night,
needing lines to swing?

I tried on faith

like a fat sister,
then I met the promised man.
He stood in the neon glamour of Friday night,
the man with the epiphany raised above
his head, uncertain as a rock.
His mouth was a tunnel and
out of his hat flew wonder, like
a dove. He was as soft as blue.

Later, I hovered in my kitchen
circle of infernal witches. They
vowed love & other breakable things.
They foretold diamonds in the dregs of my
tea-cup, and I was a believer,
at least in the rain.

For Stephen

Olympus

I hiked up the broad steep spiralling streets to a Lego-land of mansions, ranches, villas with arches, pillars, fountains, an army of one-armed Venuses poised at electric gates. I climbed this suburban Mt Olympus of neat brick upon brick and perfect, knife wet grass until the swelling winter sky hung about my head. I breathed the clouds in and out. I turned around to see the tiny-tot town, floating in mist down about the plains, as small and inconsequential as my shoe, its buildings made of cards, and beyond it, a band of sea rimming the earth, strange and dangerous grey. I picked a stick of almond blossom and began my descent, a trail of petals sailing thinly in my wake.

Magill

Families mow couch plots,
industry dents fences.
Within inches we sleep.
Strangers breathe us,
the night extorts our dreams.

I am not this town

not its steeples, black with exhaust, not its marmalade ladies
dropping shrapnel in the collection box, sorting through the
yellowed undergarments of this town's dead and musty people.
I am not the prim, dew-drop grass nor the twenty-seven varieties
of roses dropping bruised petals in shining puddles. I am not the
market full of aged cheese with green living veins nor the
supermarkets full of milk and other comforts to suck. I am not the
blue humpy hills, not the buttery light, not the blinding sand nor
the stinging sea with grinning sharks. I am not the car-yards with
plastic flags slapping the northerlies nor the piercing squeal of
buses' brakes. I am not the quiet suburbs nor the burning empty
streets, so empty that any man after dark is bad. And I am not,
am not, am not this town's Friday beery breath nor the sad man
with his hand on the breast of this town.

deaf elegies
(from virginia woolf's record store)

by robert j bloomfield

Robert was born in London and was educated near the end of a road leading to Cambridge. On leaving school he spent many years locked in a succession of dark London basements before finally arriving in Australia in 1997and becoming a writing student at the University of South Australia. Still a full-time student, Robert now divides his time between his home, overlooking the spectacular Karrara kindergarten, and a variety of exotic locations in his imagination. He is nevertheless married with three young children.

Acknowledgements

I see my poetry as a blend of nostalgia, surrealism and postmodern literary theory in practice. With this in mind, I thank my family and friends for their (sometimes unconscious) motivation and support, and I acknowledge the textual and intellectual influences of Tom Raworth, André Breton, Dylan Thomas and Stéphane Mallarmé. I am also aware of the debt that I owe to the teaching staff of the University of South Australia, and especially to my honours supervisor, Ioana Petrescu.

Contents

sniffing

good day how are ya?
i'm fine i'm good i'm well
i'm talking to myself

and

why does your little dog
have tartan bows
on its ears?

what sociable creatures we are
in our solitude
sniffing each other
the way we do

sniffing for companionship
sniffing for security
sniffing for knowledge

sniffing for reference
sniffing for pleasure
sniffing for promise

ah well ...
here comes civilization
where you can look
somebody in the eyes
and ignore them

tuesday's destination

writing well on a tuesday morning
despite it being sunday
i am absent from the author and
think of pink ribbon
key
cross
diet coke

later i see an eye that is like a tadpole of red flame
i see it from the inside
the eyebrows are a seagull
the lips are tight with
petrifying beauty

something has escaped
i feel it
reach it
want it back
reaching further
reaching blacker
playing the square strings of a square guitar
mind diverting
floating floating

floating on the frozen wave of
tuesday's destination

bagatelle

illusions rising fall on treacly ocean's swell
flown up through matter making thunder flow
suspended deep in sleep drawn coral for a cell

this thought the one thought stories speak to spell
before the blue that blooms in luminescent glow
illusions rising fall on treacly ocean's swell

the fishpecked foreshore paints a skirt on hollow shell
the mingled fingers wrapped in grasping seasalt grow
suspended deep in sleep drawn coral for a cell

as tide is bound and moonpulled tide the times compel
foamfiltered coasting by the seastring undertow
illusions rising fall on treacly ocean's swell

beneath the bitten bark the sacred grains rebel
sandrippling on the shipwreck archipelago
suspended deep in sleep drawn coral for a cell

rockresting on the limpid hand of bagatelle
scumsurge the tidy skimming tideyard urge below
illusions rising fall on treacly ocean's swell
suspended deep in sleep drawn coral for a cell

there it is in one place

there it is in one place
or sometimes in another
stillness history
changing points of reference
the walls of an empty room

my decisions are non-decisions
grooves of radical intangibility
the new mystery of the spectacle
title music
television

almost everything is almost nothing
almost everything is a variation
of what is being withheld

can i do this to a sheet of paper
or a poem?

the idea seems to fall
from listening to the ecstasy
of bright opinion

new fragments of the past

maybe this was seen before
a scene
not seen before
wiped clean
maybe we were wrong before

i am divided
i face my remains

i grasp at fragile roots
the indecision drips from my wounded heel

mind-matter spills into the gutter
spider-dust blows in secret corners
i am restless as a myth

each slab is worn by my virgin feet
my feet are altered
the slab is altered

and you appear
a face behind a curtain
your wallpaper and cat
are crystal

we both are elsewhere
relative
elusive
and impossible

the idea underscores experience
a nostalgia of the abstract
i try to leap the cracks
and as i fall
real scenes
imagined scenes
melt together into numbers
titles
darkness

the doubt has no end
it feeds on itself
and this poem remains
a fragment

letter from a cousin

i hope you will pardon me
for neglecting you so long
but if we are to understand
the evolution of the culture industries
we must start at the beginning

until death increasingly begins to haunt skulls
false needs are cultivated in people
who are delighted by a photo of a shadow
because of how much it costs

instead of being complex
and often strange
we get up and go to work
then come home and watch TV

have you made contact
with the ringleaders of the 1798 revolution?

i remain as ever
your cousin

things they told me

they told me that his face was parchment-grey,
the grisly autumn wolf and truant spark,
his devil-fur was bristling with decay
and penetrated fiercely through the dark

his eyes, they said, were closed, and yet they kept
the winter's sadness in their burnt-out lid
and flicked and clattered coldly as they wept
to blur the meaning of the tears they hid

and so he's sleeping now they like to think,
from dust to dust to sleep and dust to die,
his nightly tales of twisted myst'ry link
the rings beneath a bark that cannot lie

the voice of death waits patiently to call
the living leaf to witness its own fall

i saw nothing

i saw nothing
and yet
i saw nothing

only the bony structured wrist
and lines of titles
staring likewise at themselves
with unfamiliarity
pressed to a feather
the middle distance
is drawn wide
on the space of making

it seems to me
that i am sitting back
on whose seat
to describe this slippage

and
the rushing leaf
perspective
and triangle horizon
did something
equally unusual

i heard a train

after i heard a train
i dreamed of distant stations
where
i once dropped tears into the funnel
but never cleaned away the soot

i said 'please don't throw the lights from the window'
but you knocked me out anyway
the ticket was thick and green and mysterious
and the view of the reservoir
was filled with water
racehorses scaled the vertical slopes
of the palace gardens
the flag on the fifteenth floor was polluted
every grain smelled of the north
giants waited in the sheds
where their steam was collected in cups

arriving was unknown

we held our hats for seven years
then ordered flying saucers
to take us home

all in white

sometimes
you miss
the ball and   you laugh

      as you go
      to pick it up
      biting on the
      thin sword
and bites are in the guise of another
like an
actor
in a
dumb show
         some children thrusting their hand through the wire
           at the kodachrome faces
           of a bardot or hepburn
           in red pleated skirt
           and tennis shoes

revealing the years
that we are ordinary people
corrugated
            we march we yell we scream
            watching and being watched
            on a ritualistic screen

her smile is the contents of her praying throat
the college boys are all in white   all in white

headroom

falling down in front of henry's icons what for?
wind blowing the treetops above the car park
magpies calling each other names   'olivia' – 'olivia'
the whole time listening for skids

                    the dog barking next door
sounding like it's in my head
later someone takes it out for a walk

mozart piano sonata in c k545 (1788)

outside it's hotter than a vienna june
storms are approaching from the north
bringing hailstones from the desert
a refuse truck fires smoking grapeshot from its gut
it arcs across our bows
towards the smog that forms out in the gulf

up on the horizon a spider sail surveys the coast
the captain's brass telescope
grazes gently on the miles
'no signs of powdered wigs
or blue frock coats' she sighs
(she seems surprised)

silk handkerchiefs lie weeping
on the painted landscape
grand pianos
spread their shining wings
and feed their music to the hungry sky

the corners of the manuscripts
run rustling through the edges
of an antique fingered glove
six cannibals slice
gently through the rigging
and from the quarry on the hilltop
comes the unexpected sound
of earth's disintegration

escargots

people are tired of questions of semantics
if someone wrote it – it's literature

> (i'm not even going to reference that
> quote – these things are just 'out there')

i may abandon adverbs
he said bravely

> (may i abandon adverbs?
>> no, you may not
>> now go and sit
>> down with the others

but
on second thoughts
you may abandon the *word* adverb)

all my life
i dreamed
> of being an artist

> the freedom of expression – who cares if i fake it?

what constitutes 'artist'?
> (semantics again – see separate sheet for
> answer)

i love **big words** – they're so efficient

                                                and
            it's all about
                              efficiency
                                          these days

        no punctuation
        no capitals
        no spelling
        just a jumbled mass
                                  of letters
intertextuality has gone legit

                      i'm reading

                  in the room
                            the women come and go

nice line!
              what would i say next

                  in the room
                            the women come and go
                                      dreaming of escargots

              why go around *talking of michelangelo*
                        when you could be *dreaming of*
                      escargots?

why?

44

because michelangelo
                    has five syllables
and escargots
                    has only three

and let's face it – how many five syllable words ending in -o are there?
was joe di maggio around in those days?

no?
well
how about *pickled escargots*? (kind of you to offer)
but it's not so slick
is it?

okay
michelangelo it is
but i reserve the right
to re-interpret things because

i know every letter in that poem
                              but not necessarily
                                             in the right
                    order
(let me rephrase that)

the same sea

is
turning over
its new ideas
stretching its fingers
over the fleshy shore
shaping tomorrow's landscape
washing away
yesterday's
small death
and barnacle tattoo
lapping over the feet
with
nails outstretched
and
tearing
into my complacency

untitled (in the middle of my grated cherry)

in the middle of my grated cherry
somebody is filling a kettle

the view zooms in and out in stages
for the small round bird
that is a perfect fit for its nest

on our return we pay our respects
to a site of modern art
piles of CD cases
in a junkyard of twisted metal
and some small animals
drowning in a very shiny bucket

the hollywood hotel
is sealed in a concrete tomb
but nobody knows what happened
to all the sensitive pioneers

lost in the tempest

and that is why
i'm sitting here today
looking for a phrase
lost in the tempest
a stormy word
to feed a quiet moment
and wondering
is there still a lake for rowing
big old wooden boats
that creak
and bark their way
around a secret reedy island
with snapping oars
and water seeping through
a wormy hull?

but now we're swallowed by the grass
and sinking in the silt
like a paper ballerina
and all the creatures
and their ordered world
swirl up around our chins
the specks of life
that drift into the mouths of fish
and drift into the beaks of birds
watch sylvia unpeel
while we go drowning
water dashing out the fire
from eyes that pressed

like pearls
against the rusty signs
the flyers for the launching
of the fleet
and afternoons
that spirits sell
for dust

gilels plays the 'appassionata'

pianist is mechanic
piano is the vehicle
poet is the audience

the mechanic searches
for another strange town

the poet steps out
and
brushes the hair
of an untidy metaphor

gilels plays the *appassionata*

the audience hurls
tomorrow's reviews
onto the stage

the poet
turns the pages
with his eyes

and

the audience
re-writes the poem
in its own image

the mechanic
plays
the *appassionata*
with his secret key

the audience is the piano
pianist the vehicle
poet the mechanic

bring on the empty cameras

where are those accents now
insisting that
in every part of life
there must be something growing
or something disintegrating?

youth and beauty turn to bitter grapes
left dying on the vinewrapped
minefields of suburbia

what do i care for ruined gardens?
another stuffed body more or less
or a handful of white fur
tainted by neglected soil
such futility – you won't need that hat where *you're* going!

black painted birds stand like stilted sentries
on the swaying fence
there are one-way slits
in the castle walls
make sure you're on the *inside*

the fog skates in
across the hungry marshes
where we are sometimes joined
posing in milk-stained velvet
and writhing on the sunburned deck
for the tourists and their empty cameras

#45

did you consider the possibility
of standing in a room
of paint and canvas
surrounded by a halo
of pure knowledge

or do you prefer
to spend the winter
in the stomach of a whale
digesting freud
while freud's digesting you

over there in the two corners
is a seat
that's facing in the wrong direction
and on it
boys and violent hooded horses
write paragraphs
of sterne and stony fiction

look at the boredom in their half-closed i
as they release the crouching leopard
from his milky cage
look at their rushing wriggling values
fluorescing down the unlit road

and here comes symmetry's final fling
approaching from the ordered margin of the page

the week-end sailor poem

i'm sitting on the park bench with auden
looking out to sea
when two old masters pass by
carrying yellow buckets

auden is as dry as the summer grass
and as old as the pyramids
i tell him so
and he stands up

he goes to the water's edge
where he sees the week-end sailor
sitting in a canoe

they embrace
and crumble away
over the horizon
in the direction of america

looks like i missed the boat again
and now
i'm sitting on the park bench alone

the two old masters pass by once more
this time in the opposite direction

my edges are turning brown
just like the leaves above me
soon i will be as dry as summer grass too

kant's conception of ribbons and reins

do we have a second?
experience is impossible without it
god is etched on the fabric of the mind
with a novel by dostoyevsky
that we often cannot critique

the reddest of alerts
is stronger than no
it is the only tool we have
to explain the rationalist doom
or perform the sane act
from the false conception of the law

but the mind is within the world
it is something permanent
outside of us
we must employ the ribbons and reins
to exercise the class of ends-in-themselves

the 'i' is apprehended
we enquire about the beginning
when knowledge was counted by ambulance trips

are these the same ribbons that
radiate their own little followings?

oh to be back at virginia woolf's record store

somewhere in a box

to adopt northern customs in the south
is to tie yourself on the shoestrings of the oriental corpse
resting deaf elegies
on a pantagruelian pillow

the schemes of the unknown mother
are painted images
in caves perhaps
or in their mouths
(but only rousseau knows the answer)

i have spent today
obeying red lights
and contemplating a slippery mosaic

i feel that I am somewhere
in a box
a shaved and tilted head
awaiting the long walk
to the eclectic chair

i am deckchaired
with the seventh angel
crouched
behind the controls
with pilate's license
to kill

but the head is not my own

game

in the tattered and the irony
so in my hair
the unicorn becomes a meaning

saba
saba
insane
turn your body to face me

flower
bird
beast
mankind
garbage
end of life significance

words built to be raised from disorder

pursuing the black
beneath the white
the etched out negative
of transparent knowledge

perfection is laziness
writing is laziness

guess what
guess what
nobody can guess

hommage à stéphane mallarmé

table rounds on empty unlit pools
glass filling bottle dark the journey home
heavy standing
black beneath a wave
sand to sand returning
nightly
quietly
lawns melt into emptiness
turn the face of fingers twined
on warrior shield of wind reflected
and the pale appalling moon
where death can no longer be seen wanting

sparrow in an airport

by rob walker

Rob Walker was born in Adelaide and lives at
Cherry Gardens. His 'real job' has been as
both a classroom and specialist teacher of
Music and Drama in South Australian
government primary schools. He's been
writing 'seriously' for about 8 years, with most
of his work being published on poetry
websites (in Australia, NZ, UK, Ireland,
Canada and the US) and some in Australian,
NZ and UK print journals and anthologies.
His other interests have been music
composition (for children), community and
impro theatre, exploring other cultures and
living on his modest 'farm' with his family.
official website: users.bigpond.com/robwalker1

Acknowledgements

Poems in this collection have appeared
previously online (some as earlier versions) @
*Friendly Street, The Oracular Tree, Sidereality,
Poetry DownUnder, Indie Journal* and
Poets4Peace.

Thanks to:
• my family for everything

• Graham Rowlands for encouragement and
assistance with editing, selection and ordering
of the manuscript

• everyone at Friendly Street for your feedback
and friendship

*to Lyn with love
for keeping my feet on the ground
when my head's in the clouds*

Contents

sparrow in an airport

    it's a kind of freedom
apparently having all you want

    more than enough space
for one small sparrow

    crumbs from McDonalds
controlled climate

    yet you keep hitting glass
that invisible force separates

             you   and   sky

    flapping frustration

caged in a monument to flight

a forty nine year old child
sees his first bumblebee
kew gardens, march 2003

surely this is nature's joke?
aerodynamic enigma

fat tumbling furball of
black mohair mumbling

sotto lobby
of delegates

it disappears into a
crocus (there! suck i!)

soundz the hazard
buzzer, reversez

is this for real?!
MMMMM ... it repliezzz

waddling off through air in
its woollen tigers guernsey

ovine soliloquy, stonehenge

every day they emerge from wheeled boxes
walk under the road and come
to watch us eat grass

we don't pretend to understand it.
we are handsome, but
not excessively.

they look at the mounds
scour horizon, stand very still like us
leaving perfectly good grass untouched

they always stand over there
by those big stones

Even as I speak*

The Book, from My Publisher, is now Available
And I am Chuffed.
I am here to launch Your book by the trailerful
But first note the Pristine White Marquee, yonder, stuffed
With my own Literary Masterpiece
Which You will recognize anon since thereupon
Emblazoned is my name in 96 Font
And within its covers
Works which span my career as the Ponte
Vecchio spans the Arno   Or like Meccano
The Mathematical Bridge across the Cam
Whence in My Cambridge Years I swam
Or took the Punt
Being as I am
A lazy count –
ryman of Yours.

The Book, from My Publisher, is now Available
And I am Stoked.
My Literary and Television Fame now unassailable
No longer yoked
To the Nation which gave me Birth
In '62 I pissed off from the Antipodes of Earth
From the Land of the Shadows
Falling Towards England with Germaine and Bobby Hughes
(So much more urbane than all of Yous . . .)
From the Sinking Ship, we fled, we Rats
(Though we prefer the term Ex-Pats)
But don't forget it was We who blazed the Trail
For Edna, Kylie and her sexy tail.

The Book, from My Publisher, is now Available
And Far Be It from Me to take the piss
Yet I feel that I would be remiss
Not to make just a mention, albeit cursory
Of Your little 28th Anniversary
Most of You can barely dream but to attain
The dizzy Heights of My Poetic Reign
But we All must suffer for Our Art
Of this I make no trite apology
You Little People, sparrows picking up my verbal crumbs
Must be content with One Poem in an Anthology

The Book, from My Publisher, is now Available
And I am Rapt.
Your little selection may well be saleable
But it is apt
That I should spend my concise Flying Visit promoting My Latest Work,
A fat volume with an overstated wrapper
(Perhaps like Eminem?)
Nolite Desperare, My Nobodies:
Even a Great Man such as Myself had humble beginnings
O! The Irony of being a Republican living off Royalties, not thinning!
Even as I speak I am reposing
Yet simultaneously composing a witty poem, a critical essay on a Russian
    poet and the lyric of a Rock song, overstated.

My Book, from my Publisher, is now Available
And I am sated.

*Any resemblance between characters in this work and actual persons, living, dead,
 or just puffing a bit, is purely coincidental.*

Chester mourning

Chester morning   has broken   we swarm   from the coach   foraging
for photos and memories   while the faithful   are disembodied hymns
from other centuries   escaping a sandstone cathedral   and the unfaithful
in bed

we scavenge and   scour   emptied streets   of halftimbered
magpie buildings in   black and white   but Eleanor's
wet garden   is in full   colour like the   first dewfall on the
first grass

we look down   on rainbow-dewed paradise   a squirrel breakfasts   on
ancient Roman   city wall   and a dove   hints at peace   in Tony
Blair's Britain   and the Kentucky guy   drawls that he has
        both squirrels and doves   back home and

shoots them.

colin powell addresses the UN

it's powerpoint of course.
    all power. no point.

microsoftware
    before the macrohardware

all style   no substance
    erect an argument on flawed foundations

holes the size
    of bombcraters

a colon
    : pregnant pause before a war

lives reduced
    not to dot points

                but bullet points

eurostar

you emerge from earth's
bowels to another
country where the sun
is brighter
even grass and villages
whisper *en français*

you become obsessed
with taking THE photo
a typical landscape *au calais*
whenever background is right

a bridge jumps to foreground
at lightspeed

then you realise
everything is
typical
think fleetingly
conviction growing
you're viewing a loop
it's the same green grass,
same recurring little *église*

and all your life has been

déja-vu.

persistence of memory
Montmartre (1/4/2003)

you want to experience
le paris romantique.
Art de la rue

you enter *le métro* at *Sèvres Babylone* sardined
in the moviescene with accordion boy
and commuting extras   where is *Amélie?*

get off at *Abbesses*
all arched mausoleum
white tiles *à la morgue*

your *francais c'est terrible*
Non. Pas anglais.
you miss *la funiculaire*

climb spiral stairs up and up
(*ascenseur pour l'échafaud?*) out of breath
up and up   litter supplants people

discarded *billets* a road less travelled?
suddenly irrational anxiety knifes you
eyes crave sky   lungs fresh air

then you see her on grimy steps
locks curled as Michelangelo's David
asleep or   drugged or

dead.

panic. don't stop. must be asleep. keep moving
you step over and

up
up (wrought as iron)
up
and   out

into the light   *bienvenue*
climb *la Butte*   steep cobbled streets
to *Sacré-Cœur*

this is better. *Place du Tertre*
berets   easels   what you want
to remember

Wonderland of street artists
Toulouse-Lautrec, Picasso as you dreamed
they would be

Dali *éspace* exhibition
Salvador is now an institution
Surreal's out there   in Paris streets.

But in the middle
of night
you awake yet
to horrored guilt

see black curls
wonder who she was
dare not ask   is she   alive

in your mind   forever unconscious
             limply flowing   down those steps
                      like a melting Dali clock

Albert's Armistice
For Alby Eldridge 11/11/1896–1968

Some died in the Somme
 others, like Wilfrid, ironically
  days before Armistice.
   They lived full lives, died at twenty

Albert survived mustard gas
 with one collapsed lung,
  to half live a life
   for another 50 years

the Peace of Paper signed
 on Albert's birthday
  Kaiser sending him *eine kleine Gabe* by airmail
   a fragment of german vocab,
   'schrapnel'

which Albert exchanged for a
 Piece of Bowel

Repatriated.
 Worked for the council.
  Buried others who died.
   Cleaned floors at the Post Office.
   Retired.

Australia Post Magazine
 arrived monthly
  wearing dust at his TV table
  for years.

The TPI pension bought a chair where he lived.
 To watch through his 26" window
  the wonders of the New World
  he no longer understood.
   The TV was Healing.
   Albert wasn't.

He avoided talk of trenches, mud, blood, rats
 dying mates, shell shock, lung-eating acid
  or 'half the seed of Europe dying one by one . . .' Just
  'War's bloody stupid.'

A handsome digger before embarkation looked down
 from a dark oil painting on the paintpeeled high wall.
  Patriotism running high for King and the Mother Country.
  A saddler in a horse-redundant war.

The real grandpa sat hacking up phlegm into a coffee mug full
    of tissues

Waiting to die

The greek girl with polio

in the sixties she
had two disabilities:
cripple and *new australian*

                a teacher's guilt
                cleaving her from
                the others

as we Lined Up behind
clanking cast iron
Kframe desks

                her coathanger shoulders
                hung a pale handmade
                pink cardigan

under shapeless long dresses
badly-carved mahogany legs
of dysfunctional furniture

                she would be Dismissed first
                hobbling   callipered
                through the Guard of Dishonour

to be first out
into the sun.
To sit alone

                Stella Might Fall
                Stella Might Get Hurt
                You Don't Know How Lucky You Are

every word from a teacher's mouth
a further alienation to feed
Grade Three resentment

                        her special treatment
                        emphasised difference
                        ignored commonality

even now i share my guilt
with a teacher, long dead
whose misplaced pity

                        turned this lonely girl
                        into The Enemy.

lean
poem
pisa

stop the
presses

it's still
leaning.

10 000
came
today

they'll
all back
me up

ten
thousand
photos

of It
leaning in
albums

across the
planet

each
photo
identical

except
for that

person
in front

low ebb, high tide
Venezia, 11/03/03

fog lies thick on the *grande canale*
the launches from *mestre*
rely on radar   visibility just metres
                    vaporetti in a vapour

through air thick with fog and war
i talk to francesca our guide
of empires greek
                    roman
                            venetian

and we wonder aloud if
            this is the beginning of
                    the end of the US empire

the beginning
of the slow slide to silt

awaiting an ultimate
acqua alta

Po valley marble chips

this whole country's
on spring's cusp
slenderbranched forest
are they elm?
i'm a sclerophyte myself
each shoot in pregnant bud
any day they'll explode
and i won't be here

crosscrissing the po
in a tourist bus
the water's clean melted
snow from the alps
the rubble and gravel
purest white *carrara* marble chips
you imagine a scree at the feet
of michelangelo and David

the autobahn goes straight
through dark mountains
then flash! *snap*
a new vista
like watching the slideshow
of your holiday
while you're still
on it

beauty, dripping

undertree i am scraping
    drippings
    from the oventray with a plastic spoon

enamel baked black   specks of white
    thinnest
    coating of grease

milky way of a misted winter
    night
    the deeper groove a moon's halo

yellow fat curling from a sky
    huon
    pine shavings curving off my plane

bow waves from a boat   fogbound
    tight
    curls of that blond boy at school

and within each curl   morning sun
    catches
    numberless yellow sparkles

all this beauty
    rendered
    from death

In an overseas campaign promoting Australia, Les Murray's accent has been 'toned down' as Singaporeans have had difficulty in understanding Murray's true blue accent. Perhaps he may have to rewrite his poems as well:

The Dream of Wearing Shorts Hardly Ever

Kingdom of Flaunt this ain't.
Only Westerners flash corpulent carnal thighs
Even in this muggy clime

Our river bends are paved
Drinking water snakes in a steel
pipe across the causeway

Birds *twik twik* in virtual
Changi forests

We tolerate the *sarong*, *dhoti*, *sari*
but our real National Costume is a long white shirt,
tie and long black pants.

there's always the airconditioner

we're more Western than Westerners
who stand out on Orchard Road,
sore thumbs and dogs' balls

nothing says Aussie tourist
more than a loud *rowwll* voice
louder shirt
shorts and a hat

you can keep your green timber
we want glass and concrete,
the quality of sprawl
towards the calm sea

to look across newly reclaimed land

our great island moving
further out into the tropics

The Monkey at the Muzium
Muzium Negara *(National Museum) Kuala Lumpur Jan, 2000.*

KL megalopolis
Steaming rainforest transmuted to malls
Buttressed giants to twin stainless towers piercing humid smog

Near the centre, colonial relic museum.
Hydraulic mouth of the air-con coach
vomits up pasty tourists

filing lemminglike to pay one Ringgit each to absorb
Local culture by instant
osmosis

The Peninsula's entire Natural History
contained in thick, tiled walls.
Classified & sorted in a nineteenth century British timewarp

Traditional instruments ethnically cleansed. Imprisoned in
    glasscases.
Darkwoodstainedborders. Incarcerated at Her Majesty's pleasure.
Sentenced 'Never-to-be-released-or-played'.

The drums – now re-educated as 'Membranophones' –
Segregated from the stringed *sape*
for it is a 'Chordophone.'

Mammals, reptiles and amphibians plundered from forests
    superseded by semi-conductor factories. Doomed to stare
    eternally glass-eyed
From their jungle dioramas.

Exquisite iridescent rainbow butterflywings
Gather dust
In glass habitats

My wife returns to the bus
And with Kuma, the hindu driver,
Spots a surviving rhesus monkey swing defiantly from a banyan
High above the traffic.

But the tourists don't see it.
They're inside peering into glass cases.

Hornbill in a cage
Sarawak, Jan 2000

so this is *saved from extinction*
no sky   undulating flight
branch-branch flit   attenuated

your territory now square
catwalk mannequin
parading a cubic universe

Sam Toucan's technicolor on a cerealbox
                    you're in a box
head blooming like a strelitzia

bird-of-paradise
– become –
bird-of-hell

Orange man
Semengoh Orang Utan Rehabilitation Centre,
Sarawak, Malaysia

freed, he is drawn back
    stuck in welfare's cycle

venture to Wide World
    return to soup kitchen

it's hard going straight
    when your mate's

in the slammer.
    old recidivist back again

tries to mate
    through bars

accepts prison grub
    from his in-mate

        sadness in her eyes
            shows
            she knows

                the origins of

                extinction.

Unity

We hold hands

a gathering
together

to unite
against
Other

the closer
Our circle

the more
You
are
excluded

the more
We become
Us

the more
You
become
Them

detention
14/8/2001

My name is Shayan
  I live in the middle of your city
Behind the razor wire.
I am 8. My parents ran from iran
  Iran too
Now we are locked up in Villawood.
  It's a pretty name isn't it?
They say that Australia is a beautiful country
  I don't know.
I've only seen the huts

  and the razorwire

I don't eat any more.

Sumatran tiger
Adelaide Zoo, Jan 2004

measures a synthetic jungle
in paces   twenty up
                   twenty back

fluidly lithe even in
                 contained repetition

sniffs air discovers sushi
imagines fish in a wild river   a
                 lightning pounce

but for this mesh could
bring down a hairless primate just
                 for practice

frowns. tries to remember
a jungle it has
                 never known

The Impressionists
– a reflection on an exhibition
NGV, July 2004

We queue to be impressed
At first we are not impressed
that it opens half an hour late

this forces us to queue unimpressed
of a Melbourne winter's morning
until the sun (an emerging poet)

does a good impression of
Paris au printemps and we
are forced to reflect on
                and in

the wall of water which could
have been done by Manet

and the impressionable little girl
In the pink parka wide-eyes
the reflections

pressing tentative fingers
and her mother gives her a book
Katie meets the Impressionists

but what impresses this little girl is
shining on a shimmering vertical plane
in this urban winter balm

and what may be the impression
of this day in years to come
will not be pictures in golden ratio frames

but a morning Melbourne sun
quivering on a glass wall
of water.